About this book

The First World War began in August 1914 and continued until the end of 1918. Growing up during this time was sometimes a bewildering and frightening experience. Nearly every child in Britain, Germany, France and Belgium, and other countries, lost a father, brother, or other relative on the battlefield.

At first the War had seemed an exciting and adventurous prospect. But as the years passed and the number of casualties mounted, and food and clothing became scarce, everyone grew depressed and weary. In wars before 1914 only people living in the battle areas had been affected, but in the First World War everyone suffered hardships. The War was a disaster for the victors as well as for the conquered peoples. This book tells you a little about what it was like to be a child in those days.

There are more than fifty photographs taken at the time, and the book includes a glossary, a reading list and an index.

Growing up
in the
First World War

PHILIP WARNER

Growing up in Other Times

Frontispiece: This is what a great many children in Britain looked like in 1914. In those days most people were much poorer than we are now.

ISBN 0 85340 761 4

First published in 1980 by Wayland Publishers Ltd,
49 Lansdowne Place, Hove, East Sussex BN3 1HF, England
2nd impression 1983

Text set in 12 pt. VIP Univers by Trident Graphics Limited,
Reigate, Surrey
Printed and bound in Great Britain
at the Pitman Press, Bath

Contents

1 The Opening Stages

The War began in August 1914, when Germany invaded Belgium on the way to attack France. Britain had signed an agreement to defend Belgium and so the British Empire — as it was then — was brought into the War, with Canada, Australia, India, and many other countries coming in on the side of the Allies. The Allies were Britain, France and Russia, and against them were Germany, Austria, Bulgaria and Turkey, who were called the Central Powers. Later Italy joined the Allies.

At the outbreak of war there was great enthusiasm, and most people believed that the Germans would soon be beaten and the fighting would end before Christmas. Many young men, and some older ones too, hurried to join up, so that they could take part in the fighting before it was all over. The picture opposite shows a great crowd cheering King George V and Queen Mary at the beginning of the War.

The Germans quickly showed that this would not be a war confined to the battlefields. A German plane dropped a bomb on Dover on Christmas Eve 1914. A greater threat came from airships, which could carry a large quantity of bombs. In December 1914 German ships crossed the North Sea and shelled towns on the east coast of Britain, killing and injuring several people.

These acts against civilians gave the British people a great feeling of patriotism and determination to beat the Germans soundly and quickly.

Opening the sluices

To delay the German advance through Belgium, the sluice gates which held back the North Sea were opened to allow the land to become flooded. This made it

difficult for the advancing German armies, but it did not delay them for long. The flooding left parts of Belgium covered in shallow water, where children could play happily, as you can see here.

The Kitchener poster This picture of Lord
Kitchener is the most famous recruiting poster of
the War. Kitchener was a great soldier and
statesman. He did not believe that the fighting
would end quickly, and he therefore made plans to
raise huge armies in preparation for a long war.
He was drowned in 1915 when a ship on which he
was travelling was hit by a mine, so he never saw
the results of his foresight. The picture above
shows young men besieging a recruiting office.
The official minimum age for a soldier was 18 but
some youngsters were so keen to join up that they
lied about their age.

Children recruiting Even children joined
in the recruiting drive. These boys, giving a
demonstration in Trafalgar Square, are encouraging men to join the army. They might be members
of the Boys' Brigade although they are not wearing their familiar pill-box hats.

German propaganda The Germans too tried to build up a warlike spirit in their people. In this cartoon from a magazine the devil is roasting John Bull in hell. John Bull is offering the devil a bag of money to try to stop him! The message is, 'May God Punish England'.

Anti-German riots Many Germans had, over the years, settled in Britain and become British citizens. However, after the outbreak of war, people with German names were often suspected of being spies. Shops with German names were sometimes broken into, and you can see in this picture that the lower windows of the German shop have been boarded up, and upstairs they have been smashed with stones. Even children were caught up in this anti-German feeling — perhaps some of the children in the picture broke the windows.

Belgian refugees As the Germans
marched into their country, pillaging towns and
taking prisoners, many Belgians escaped and
came to Britain. Their unhappy situation helped to
gain support from the British people against the
Germans. This group of refugees has just arrived
at Victoria Station, and many of them were taken
into British homes. They would not see their own
homes again for four years.

2 Fighting on the Battle Front

After the first German onslaught had been thrust back by the Allied armies, both sides dug themselves into trenches. These trenches were to protect the soldiers against enemy gunfire, and they stretched across Europe from the French coast to Switzerland — over 650 kilometres. Thousands of lives would be lost between the lines of trenches just to gain a few hundred metres, and those few hundred metres could easily be lost again the following day. One soldier here is writing a last letter home before an attack while his comrades snatch a few moments of sleep.

Although the heaviest fighting took place in the trenches in France, there were many battles in other parts of the world too. Poland was the scene of a great battle between the Russian and German armies soon after the beginning of the War, when the Russian army was heavily defeated. There was fighting too in Africa, Palestine, Iraq, Greece, Austria, and Serbia (which is now a part of Yugoslavia).

But it is the trenches that will always be remembered as the typical battleground of the First World War.

An amazing charge This scene looks as if it could only have taken place in the pages of a boy's comic. But it really happened. The picture appeared in the *Illustrated London News* for 29th July 1916. The story explained that the captain of the East Surrey Regiment had the idea of encouraging his men to kick a football as they charged an enemy trench. Obviously it was to take their minds off the danger from shell-bursts and

machine-gun fire. There were four footballs altogether; you can see two of them in the picture. After kicking the footballs for nearly two kilometres they successfully occupied the German trench, and later recovered two of the footballs for their regimental museum. It was the sort of story which made people back home think of the War as a glorious thing, but for the soldiers at the Front the charge was definitely not a game.

Russian soldiers The Russians had a very large army. It included soldiers of all ages. Unfortunately the Russian army was very badly equipped, and there were not enough rifles for everyone. Early in the War, two huge Russian armies were defeated in Poland. The picture shows how young some of their soldiers were.

Children at the Front Some French
families lived very close to the front line, and
occasionally children would wander too near.
These two little French girls have made friends
with a British military policeman, who is taking
them to a safer place. They are wearing 'tin hats'
(helmets) to protect their heads.

Gas masks Poison gas, a deadly weapon, was used by both sides on the battle front. These French schoolchildren are practising wearing gas masks. Fortunately gas was never used in the bombing of towns.

Air raids in France The German air force quite often bombed French cities. This picture shows a group of young children and babies with their nurses, who have taken refuge in a cellar to escape from the bombs during an air raid over Rheims, a town in northern France.

Trading with the soldiers These British soldiers are staying in a French village which has been recaptured from the Germans. A local girl is trying to sell chocolate to them. But chocolate is expensive in wartime, and the soldiers do not look very interested in parting with their money. You can see from her shoes that the girl is very poor.

Greek refugees The families in this picture are refugees who have fled to Salonika, a northern province of Greece. They have escaped from German and Bulgarian troops. Forty thousand refugees, including many children, lived in these tents provided by the British, and they endured great hardship during very cold winter weather.

The wounded return Children in England soon began to understand what the War meant when they watched ambulances collecting the wounded from Charing Cross and other big

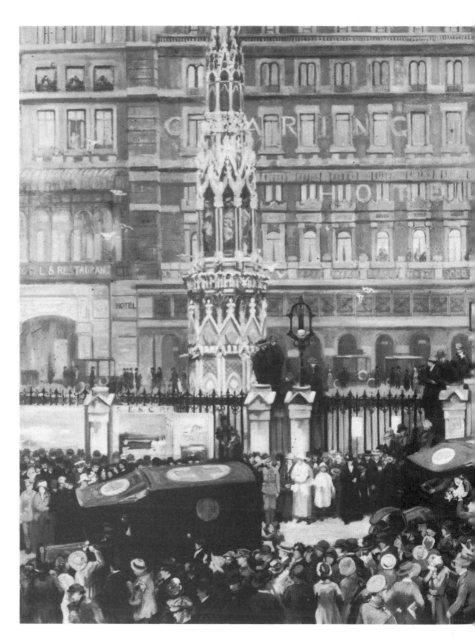

London stations. The men had been brought there from the battlefields of France. Now they would have time to rest in hospital. But as soon as they were fit they would be sent back to the Front.

3 Life at Home

As the war years dragged on, the early excitement amongst the people at home gradually changed to sadness and grim resolution. They began to realize that it would be a long and costly war.

As the lists of dead and wounded grew longer there were calls for more and more men to take their place. All fit men between the ages of eighteen and forty-five years could expect to be called up. There were a few exceptions – essential farmworkers, and men with very special skills working in factories, would not be called up. Whenever possible women took over work which had been done by men. They worked in factories and on farms, drove buses and lorries, even became lumberjacks. Children also, in their spare time, did all sorts of jobs they would never have done in peacetime.

Everybody was very careful not to waste anything. Many foods and other essential items were in very short supply because they had to be brought to Britain from overseas. The ships bringing those goods took a long time, and were often sunk by submarines. Before the end of the War foods such as bread, meat, butter, and sugar were rationed so that everyone had a fair share.

The picture opposite shows relatives waiting for news of soldiers missing at the Front. A special room was provided at the War Office where they could go for news. A boy scout is helping to take messages.

'Old Contemptibles' This was a sight that stirred the heart of every British child — soldiers marching through town on their way to the Front. Notice how they nearly all have moustaches, which were very fashionable in those days. The German emperor, the 'Kaiser', had referred to Britain's 'contemptible little army'. But it was this army which checked the German advance at the Battle of Mons. From then on they were nicknamed 'the old contemptibles'.

Air raid on London There were very few air raids during the First World War, but when they did occur they caused great fear and distress. The Germans sent over aeroplanes and sometimes enormous airships called Zeppelins (you can see a Zeppelin on pages 50–51). When these dropped bombs and killed people, Londoners were shocked and bewildered. This picture shows children who suffered a direct bomb on their school one morning. They are being carried out by policemen and firemen.

Future soldiers This picture shows Eton schoolboys wearing their school uniform as they march through the town. They are members of the Officer Training Corps. These boys trained to be army officers while still at school. They would be sent straight to the battlefields on leaving school and many would be killed at the Front before the end of the War.

Growing their own As the War continued there was a shortage of food because enemy ships and submarines prevented food reaching Britain from overseas. This was called a blockade. People were encouraged to grow as much food of their own as possible, in gardens and allotments. Here you see schoolgirls hard at work, digging and planting vegetables.

Boy scouts Boy scouts did very useful work during the War. In the hospitals they distributed food, scrubbed floors, and posted letters. Here they are taking some wounded soldiers for an airing. Their shorts were very long in those days, and look rather comical to us — but it was scouts who began the fashion of wearing shorts for sport and outdoor recreation. In the picture opposite you can see scouts helping to harvest flax. The seeds were used for making linseed oil, and the stalks were used for making linen.

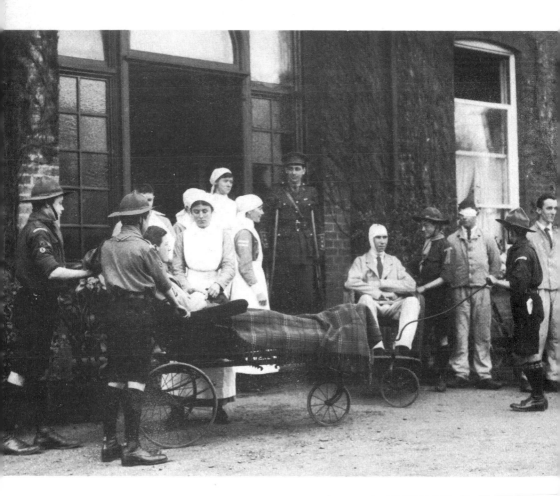

35

Rolling bandages Bandages were desperately needed for all the wounded, and they had to be rolled so that they could be applied easily and quickly. Here the job is being done by girl guides, using special rollers.

Making clothes in school Even young children helped in the war effort, by sewing clothes. Clothing factories were very busy making uniforms and other important items for the forces, and materials were scarce, so these children helped by mending clothes for themselves and their friends.

Women doing 'men's work'

During the War women took over many jobs which had formerly been done only by men. They became bus drivers and conductors, coalheavers, and farmworkers, so that the men who normally did this work were free to join the forces. Here are two women forestry workers, sharpening an axe on a grindstone.

In the past, only poor women had worked in factories. But now with the country at war many more women joined them and some became skilled mechanics, craftsmen, and engineers. Here you see women making propellers for the aeroplanes, which were mostly made of wood.

A young farmworker The normal school-leaving age was fourteen. This fourteen-year-old Cornish girl, pictured above, is not merely working, however; she has already won prizes for her skill in ploughing. Nearly all ploughing was done by horses in those days.

Collecting salvage Guns, ships, and ammunition required huge quantities of metal and other materials. Very little was allowed to go to waste. In this picture children are helping by collecting metal pots and pans, timber, and any other materials which the factories could use, from a rubbish dump.

Haybox cooking When wood and fuel were in short supply everyone tried to use the most economical ways of cooking. Here a haybox cooker is being demonstrated to show how — after a stew has been warmed up — it can continue to simmer for hours in a box filled with hay, which conserves heat. A lot of fuel could be saved in this way.

Children's canteens As the War dragged on and on, supplies of food in Britain dwindled further. In order to ensure that children were properly fed, public canteens were opened where children could get a nourishing meal quite cheaply. These children in Kent are eating their midday meal in a patriotically decorated canteen run by volunteers.

Queues
As a result of the food shortages, long queues would form outside any shop which had recently received fresh supplies. Many staple foods such as meat, bread, butter and sugar were

in short supply. In one shop window in this picture is a notice saying, 'England Expects Economy'. The two lines running down the cobbled street are tram rails, which are rarely seen in Britain now.

The Red Cross England was not the only country short of food. Other countries were blockaded too. This picture shows Red Cross supplies being handed out to eagerly waiting Italian children. Throughout the War the Red Cross continued its humanitarian efforts to bring relief from suffering to all people, whatever side they were on.

London in wartime This was an unusual scene in Regent's Park. The little girl would long remember the strange shapes of the big buildings put up by the Royal Air Force. All the great London parks were used by the Forces for drilling, training and storage.

4 The Naval and Air War

The naval war took place in the Atlantic, Pacific and Mediterranean seas. The German fleet included many submarines, called U-boats, which lay in wait to attack Allied shipping, but their main battle fleet came into contact with the British Grand Fleet only once, at the Battle of Jutland in 1916.

John Cornwell was 16½ years old when his ship H.M.S. *Chester* took part in that great battle. He was badly wounded, but stayed at his gun even after the rest of the crew had been killed or wounded. The picture shows him at his post awaiting orders, although hardly able to stand because of his mortal wounds. He died while still at the gun, and after his death was awarded the Victoria Cross for his courage.

The air forces of both sides were at first mainly used to watch the movements of enemy armies on the ground, and to direct artillery fire. However, the pilots soon realized that in order to prevent their rivals reporting back the information they had observed, they had to shoot them down. Fighting in the air then developed and aeroplanes, although primitive, became faster and more man-oeuvrable. The pilots were superbly daring and skilful, especially in handling their aeroplanes during 'dog fights', when they would try by all means to shoot their opponents down. These pilots became known as 'air aces'. Many of them were killed before the end of the War.

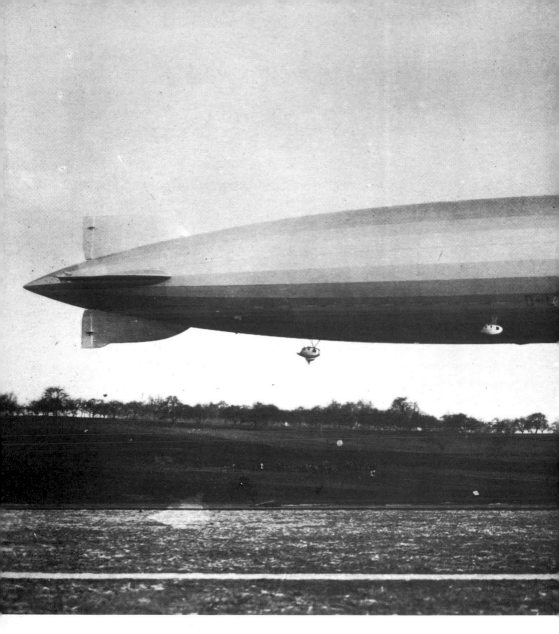

German airships

Imagine you came out of your house one morning and saw a spaceship from another planet hovering over the back garden. That is how children must have felt when they saw the first Zeppelin airships. These enormous sausage shapes were often to be seen in the air over Britain, creating great panic. But although

their bombs caused a great deal of destruction, they were slow and could not fly very high. In 1916 the British were able to shoot them down with a special bullet which set fire to the gas which propelled the giant airships. The enormous fire following the shooting down of a Zeppelin could be seen for miles.

'Dog fights'

This sort of scene became a familiar sight to children, especially over France. The aerial battles which took place when Allied and German planes encountered each other were called 'dog fights'. The German planes are marked with black crosses, and the British planes with roundels of red, white and blue.

Hero of the air

Pilots were at their best when young, when their eyesight was keen and their reactions quick. Sadly, many of them did not live very long. Captain Albert Ball is shown opposite. Only seventeen when the War started, he was killed at the age of twenty. By that time he had destroyed forty-three German aircraft and won the Victoria Cross, the Distinguished Service Order, and the Military Cross.

Sinking of the 'Lusitania'

These two little girls, reading quietly with their mother on the deck of a magnificent ocean liner, are unaware of an impending tragedy. But other people are staring in horror at a torpedo streaking towards them through the water. The *Lusitania* was a British passenger liner, which sailed regularly between Liverpool and New York. Because of its high speed it was believed to be safe from submarine attack. However, on 7th May 1915 U-boat torpedoes struck the ship when it was a few miles from the Irish coast, and it sank so quickly that over a thousand passengers were drowned. Many of them were American, and this act of aggression greatly influenced American public opinion in favour of the Allied cause.

5 The Final Stages

In the spring of 1918 the Germans made a supreme effort and broke through the Allied lines. However, after desperate fighting they were stopped just before they crushed the last lines of resistance. After that the German effort was exhausted, and gradually they were pushed back by the Allies. By that time they realized they had no hope of winning the War.

At 11.00 a.m. on 11th November 1918 the German army surrendered to the Allies in what was called the Armistice. Now the real cost of the War — the loss of life of almost an entire generation of young men — could be counted. The picture opposite reflects the feelings of the bereaved families. Shrines like these were sometimes set up in the streets of villages and towns.

Besides those killed there were a great number of people who had been very badly injured. Some soldiers returned so crippled that they could never again lead a normal life. Others had lost limbs, or had been affected by gas and disease, and there were some whose nerves had been utterly shattered.

However, at the Armistice all was rejoicing. In the victorious countries men, women and children danced and sang in the streets. Their joy was in the relief of knowing that the terrible slaughter would now stop.

Enlisting for Uncle Sam When the United States came into the War in 1917 they called for volunteers to join the army. Huge numbers of men came to the recruiting offices. This picture shows them lining up in order to enlist in the United States Army, eager to travel to Europe and do battle with the Germans. 'Uncle Sam' is a patriotic nickname for the United States, like 'John Bull' is for Britain.

New York American

WAR WITH GERMANY

Tanks Before the First World War, tanks were only found in science fiction stories by authors like H. G. Wells. When the first tanks were introduced it was hoped that the trench war might end, and the troops would be able to make a big advance. The first tanks weighed twenty-eight tonnes, had a speed of only four miles per hour, (6.5 km/h) and kept breaking down. Despite these problems they were used because their great weight enabled them to break through enemy barbed wire without exposing the soldiers to gunfire.

Liberation As the tide of victory began to turn, the Germans started to retreat. Imagine the joy of people, whose country had been occupied for four years, when they saw the Allies arrive to rescue them. Here Belgians are welcoming the arrival of British troops who have liberated the town of Ostend.

But liberation did not always mean the end of suffering. These French people have returned to their liberated village after the Battle of Cambrai in 1917, and have found it in ruins. The tide of war has turned for them, but it will be years before their village will be properly rebuilt, and their prosperity restored.

Getting together Here is another of the German 'God punish England' notices (you saw one on page 13). This one was painted on the door of a warehouse during the occupation of a Belgian village. Now the Allies have liberated the village, and for a joke some soldiers have decided to pose in front of it for a photograph. They are accompanied by people of the village. Everyone is grinning cheerfully, and most of the children have been given soldiers' helmets to wear.

The battleground In 1914 there was a beautiful forest at St Quentin, in France, where children played and families came for picnics. This is what it looked like in 1918. Trees, blasted by gunfire, stick up from the stagnant pools of rain-water and mud which collected in the craters of shell-bursts and in the trenches. This scene stretched for hundreds of kilometres through France and Belgium, and it was many years before the countryside was restored to its former beauty.

The Armistice The War ended at the eleventh hour of the eleventh day of the eleventh month of 1918. There was wild rejoicing on both sides of the Atlantic and people danced in the streets for joy. Ever since, the Sunday nearest to the 11th November each year has been the official day of remembrance for the dead. The pictures show happy W.R.A.F.s (members of the Women's Royal Air Force) cheering, and, in New York, victory being celebrated by cheering crowds with waving flags and streaming ticker-tape.

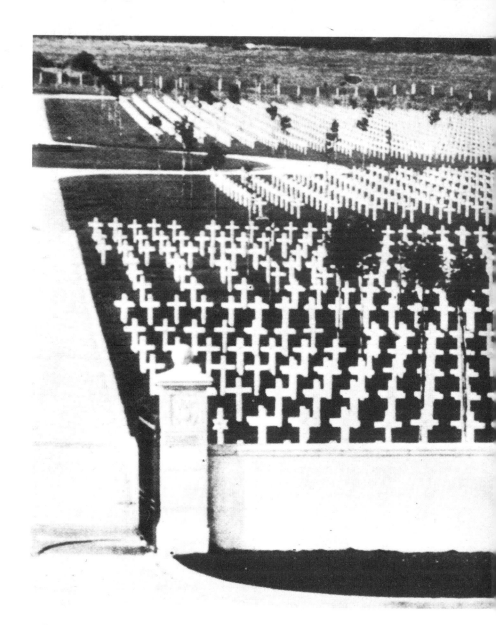

The lost generation But the cost of this terrible war had to be reckoned in lives and in destruction. There are war cemeteries like this one in many parts of the world, especially in France. The body of one unknown soldier was buried in Westminster Abbey in London, and others in the

capital cities of many countries all over the world.
These memorials to 'unknown soldiers' remind us of
the millions who died and had no grave — all those
husbands, sons, and fathers, who are remembered
now only by the old. But on Remembrance Sunday
every November we too commemorate their deaths.

New Words

Artillery	Large guns, and the branch of the army that uses these guns.
Barrage	Continuous heavy gunfire.
Blockade	Blocking the approaches to a country by land or sea, in order to prevent supplies getting through.
Casualty	Someone who is killed, wounded, captured or missing as a result of war.
Dog fight	Aerial combat between fighter planes.
Infantry	Foot soldiers; soldiers who fight on foot with hand weapons.
John Bull	The symbol of England and the English people.
Patriotic	To be inspired by love of one's country.
Propaganda	The spreading of both true and false information to assist one side in a war and damage the enemy's side.
Recruiting	Persuading people to join one of the fighting services.
Refugee	Someone who seeks shelter in another country to escape from danger.
Salvage	To collect and save items which have been thrown away, and which could be used in factories to help the war effort.

Sluice	A gate or dam to control the flow of water — used especially in Holland and Belgium, where much of the land is below sea-level.
Ticker-tape	Paper ribbon used in offices in New York, and traditionally thrown from windows at times of festivity.
Trenches	Long, deep ditches dug by soldiers to protect themselves from enemy gunfire.
U-boats	German submarines.
Zeppelins	German airships, named after their inventor, Count von Zeppelin.

More Books

Battle of the Somme by Christopher Martin (Wayland)

How We Used to Live 1908–1918 (Macdonald Educational)

The Great War Causes and Consequences by Duncan MacIntyre (Blackie)

The Origins of World War I by Roger Parkinson (Wayland)

War in the Trenches by Michael Holden (Wayland)

World War One by Robert Hoare (Macdonald Educational)

Index

Picture acknowledgements

BBC Hulton Picture Library, frontispiece, pages 12, 14, 35; Imperial War Museum, 15, 16, 21, 22–3, 24, 25, 33, 34, 36, 37, 38, 39, 41, 43, 44–5, 46–7, 59, 60, 61, 62; Mansell Picture Library, 6, 8–9, 11, 20, 49, 54, 55, 65; Nottingham Museum, 53; Popperfoto, 64; Philip Warner, 13, 23, 32, 40, 46, 52, 56, 57, 63, 66–7.
The remaining pictures are from Wayland Picture Library.